An illustrated souvenir

BEATRIX POTTER
AND HILL TOP

Cumbria

Judy Taylor

The National Trust

Beatrix Potter and Hill Top

On 10 October 1905 Beatrix Potter wrote from the Lake District to Frederick Warne, the publisher of her 'little books' in London: 'My purchase seems to be regarded as a huge joke; I have been going over my hill with a tape measure.' That summer she had bought Hill Top, a working farm in the village of Near Sawrey that nestled behind the local inn, the Tower Bank Arms, under the shelter of a small hill. Beatrix had travelled to Sawrey from her uncle's house in North Wales to discuss the farm with the manager, John Cannon, and to start work on making a garden. She had only a few weeks before she must return to her responsibilities in London.

To the casual observer Beatrix's cares were few. Approaching forty she was a successful author, with her sixth book, *The Tale of Mrs Tiggy-Winkle* (1905), published the previous month and already a bestseller, and the next, *The Pie and The Patty-Pan* (1905) due out in only a few days. But Beatrix was suffering a dreadful grief. Less than seven weeks before, her fiancé, Norman Warne, had died swiftly and without warning of pernicious anaemia. Their engagement had been short – and against her parents' wishes.

The Potters were an austere couple: he was a wealthy barrister, man-about-town and remarkable amateur photographer; she a strict parent and a dedicated hostess. The care of their two children, Helen Beatrix and Walter Bertram, had been entrusted to nannies and governesses – in Beatrix's case her entire education had been conducted at home – and the children had been encouraged to paint and draw at every opportunity, for they both showed early artistic talent. When they grew up Beatrix and Bertram were expected to marry advantageously or to remain at home in Bolton Gardens, West London, to supervise the care of their parents in old age.

Every April the family spent two or three weeks at the seaside while the spring-cleaning was done; every summer they rented a house in the country for a three-month holiday. The adults fished and shot and entertained their friends. The children explored the countryside and drew and painted everything they saw. After many years of holidaying in Scotland, the Potters transferred their allegiance to the Lake District and they stayed there regularly after first renting Wray Castle in 1882 when Beatrix was sixteen.

Norman Warne

Beatrix Potter, aged 8,
with her parents

'Sawrey under snow, March 7, 1909'
by Beatrix Potter

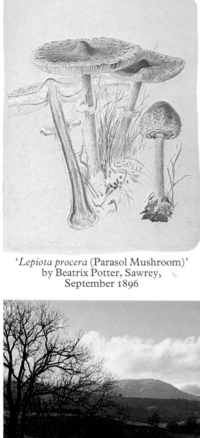

'*Lepiota procera* (Parasol Mushroom)'
by Beatrix Potter, Sawrey,
September 1896

It was taken for granted that the two young Potters would continue to accompany their parents on holiday even when they were grown-up, and Beatrix was nearly thirty when they all went to Sawrey for the first time in July 1896. The property that Rupert Potter took that year on the edge of the village was a large country house, Lakefield, which by their return in 1900 had been renamed Eeswyke or 'house on the shore'. From the pretty garden there was the magnificent view over Esthwaite Water to the hills of Coniston beyond, and behind the attractive white-washed house was a bustling farm with sheep and cows and pigs. Beatrix took her pet rabbit, Peter, with her, the coachman took his cat, and during their stay Beatrix and Bertram drew and painted, went for long walks on the fells or drove round the district in the pony and trap. It was an ideal place for Beatrix to expand her newly acquired interest in fungi and she made detailed studies of the specimens she found in the local woods.

The view over Esthwaite today
(*Mike Williams*)

'Lakefield, a walled garden, 1900'
by Beatrix Potter

4

When the time came for them to return to London Beatrix had quite fallen in love with it all. 'It is as nearly perfect a little place as I ever lived in, and such nice old-fashioned people in the village . . . Perhaps my most sentimental leave-taking was with Don, the great farm collie. He came up and muddied me as I was packing up Peter Rabbit at the edge of dark. I accompanied him to the stable-gate, where he turned, holding it open with his side, and gravely shook hands. Afterwards, putting his paws solemnly on my shoulder, he licked my face and went away into the farm.' Beatrix resolved that one day, somehow, part of this beautiful countryside would belong to her.

'Kep, March 5, 1909'
by Beatrix Potter

Lakefield (Eeswyke) in August 1896
(Rupert Potter)

Beatrix had to wait nine years before the opportunity came. The sales of *The Tale of Peter Rabbit* (1902) were prodigious – 50,000 copies in two years – and with her royalties from this, from *The Tale of Squirrel Nutkin* (1903), *The Tailor of Gloucester* (1903), and four more of her little books, she bought Hill Top Farm, the sale being completed in November 1905. It was a turning point in Beatrix's life, the start of her deep interest in farming and of her lifelong concern for the preservation and care of the land. Once Hill Top Farm was really hers she asked John Cannon to stay on as manager, while she returned to London – and planned how soon she could decently get back to Sawrey again.

Beatrix Potter in 1913 with her newly-hatched ducklings

Hill Top *c.*1912
(Rupert Potter)

Hill Top today *(Alex Black)*

Over the next few years Beatrix spent as much time as she could in Sawrey, frequently travelling up and down from London in the train. She found the air exhilarating and always slept soundly after a day working in the garden. Her health improved dramatically, as she wrote to a friend: 'I feel so very well and eating so much that I am almost ashamed of my appetite.' At first there was not room for her to stay in Hill Top itself with the Cannons and their two children, so she lodged in the village with the Satterthwaites at Belle Green, while alterations were made to the house. A small wing was added, a new dairy built and the carriage road widened and straightened. Beatrix filled the garden with cuttings and plants from newly-made acquaintances in the village and she agreed that Mrs Cannon should get some cats to cope with a sudden invasion of rats. When the house was ready for her Beatrix turned her attention to the farm, making plans with John Cannon to purchase new stock. Within two years Hill Top Farm had ten cows, fourteen pigs, some ducks and hens, and over thirty Herdwick sheep, a breed native to the Lake District with wool prized for its hard-wearing and waterproof qualities. And with the sheep came the sheepdogs, the first of Beatrix's collies, called Kep.

Beatrix Potter in the garden
of Hill Top, May 1913
(Rupert Potter)

Hill Top kitchen today
(Geoffrey Frosh)

Hill Top kitchen c.1908
(Beatrix Potter)

From *The Tale of Mr. Jeremy Fisher*

They were busy years for Beatrix but it was an ideal way for her to come to terms with her fiancé's death. As well as putting the house and farm in order, and whether she was in London or at Hill Top, she was producing new books, and her stories were starting to reflect her new enthusiasm. *The Tale of Mr. Jeremy Fisher* (1906), though begun many years earlier in Scotland, was now set on Esthwaite Water. *The Tale of Tom Kitten* (1907) clearly takes place in the house and garden of Hill Top. *The Tale of Jemima Puddle-Duck* (1908) was based on a real straying duck from Hill Top, Mrs Cannon and her children appear in the opening pictures, and the whole book is full of the farm, the village and the surrounding country. Beatrix used the farmhouse at Hill Top as the setting for *The Roly-Poly Pudding* (1908) – now called *The Tale of Samuel Whiskers* – and she even chose the invasive rats as her main characters. *The Tale of Ginger and Pickles* (1909) is very much a Sawrey book, with the old Smithy Lane village shop (now a private house) as its centre-piece. Mr Tod and Tommy Brock in *The Tale of Mr. Tod* (1912) both live in the hills around Sawrey 'at the top of Bull Banks, under Oatmeal Crag'. *The Tale of Pigling Bland* (1913), as well as featuring two of the pigs from Hill Top, has a number of pictures of the farm and the frontispiece shows the signpost at the crossroads outside the village.

From *The Tale of Mr. Tod*

The crossroads at Sawrey
(Mike Williams)

From *The Tale of
Jemima Puddle-Duck*

From *The Tale of Pigling Bland*

From *The Tale of
Samuel Whiskers*

The dresser at Hill Top,
September 1912 *(Rupert Potter)*

The rhubarb patch at
Hill Top today *(Robert Thrift)*

'The crossroads at Sawrey',
by Beatrix Potter

T. Askew's cart in Sawrey
in the early 1900s

From *The Tale of
Ginger and Pickles*

William Heelis at Hill Top

Beatrix's parents were tolerant of their daughter's new acquisition but they were not entirely sympathetic to her absence from the family home in Bolton Gardens, and they were certainly reluctant to go to Sawrey with her unless it was time for the annual summer holiday. Beatrix had been adding to her property whenever she could, buying land to extend her holding when it became available. In May 1909 she bought a second farm in Sawrey, Castle Farm, its fields conveniently marching with the Hill Top land.

In all her property dealings she had taken the advice of a firm of local solicitors, W.H. Heelis & Son of Ambleside and Hawkshead and she was looked after there by the partner specialising in property and land contracts, William Heelis. As well as apprising her of future sales and arranging purchases on her behalf, he kept an eye on her property and supervised alterations and building work. He was soon intrigued by the shy but determined woman from London and he enjoyed her growing appreciation of the part of the world in which he had been born and brought up. She, in turn, was attracted to this good-looking man in his early forties with his quiet and courteous manner. She admired him, too, for the obvious respect in which he

'A row of trees in Sawrey'
by Beatrix Potter

'A view from Sawrey overlooking Esthwaite Water'
by Beatrix Potter

was held in the district. His letters to her in London helped to sustain her through the increasing disagreements with her parents. When she told them that Mr Heelis had asked her to marry him, their reaction was predictable. They were getting old and increasingly ill; their forty-six-year-old daughter's duty was to remain at home. It took Beatrix nearly a year to persuade her parents to change their minds but persuade them she did and on 15 October 1913 she and Willie were married in London. Without delay they travelled up to Sawrey to start a new life together in the Lake District.

The Heelises chose Castle Cottage as their home rather than Hill Top, Beatrix being reluctant to alter her beloved house once again. They enlarged Castle Cottage by building on to the side, and it was more private there than it would have been living cheek by jowl with the Cannons. Beatrix, however, kept Hill Top exactly as it had always been and she used it as her studio and study, and as a place to entertain her 'book visitors', an increasing number of whom were from America. At Hill Top she kept her favourite pieces of china and furniture and it was there that she stored her precious drawings.

Beatrix Potter and William Heelis October 14, 1913, the day before their wedding (*Rupert Potter*)

From *The Tale of Pigling Bland*

Castle Cottage, Sawrey, now a private dwelling (*Mike Williams*)

Beatrix's life with Willie took on a pattern that was to change little for the next thirty years. While Willie continued in his practice from the solicitors' office in Hawkshead, and served for many years as Clerk to the Justices there and at Ambleside and Windermere, Beatrix concentrated on farming and the family. Her father died soon after their marriage and she brought her mother to Sawrey from London, installing her with a companion in a furnished house in the village. The First World War made difficulties for farmers, with the constant threat of the horses being taken to the Front and the men being called up at ploughing time, but Beatrix managed it all, even working in the fields herself at harvest time. She learned quickly about the buying of stock and the breeding of sheep, and she helped to feed the calves and the pigs. She reared the turkeys and the hens and waged a constant battle to keep out marauding foxes.

Life, however, was not all hard work. Willie was a keen golfer and bowler, and he much enjoyed a day's shooting. He was an enthusiastic country and folk dancer and Beatrix often accompanied him to the neighbouring village dances, she to observe and to draw rather than to dance. Although she was always under pressure from her publishers for a new book, she was suffering from eye strain and she found it difficult to combine authorship with all her other commitments. She produced only four more of her little books after her marriage to Willie. One of them, *The Tale of Johnny Town-Mouse* (1918), she set very clearly in the narrow streets and alley ways of nearby Hawkshead.

With the war over, Beatrix bought a house for her mother on the other side of Lake Windermere. In the same year, with her characteristic concern for the neighbourhood, she set up the Hawkshead and District Nursing Association to provide a district nurse for the villages in the area. But it was into her farming that she put most of her energies. In 1924 she bought one of the most spectacularly situated farms in the Lake District, Troutbeck Park Farm in the Troutbeck Valley near Windermere. The farm was in poor shape but its extensive land offered her the opportunity to expand her sheep flocks and to breed her favourite Herdwicks. She engaged Tom Storey as her shepherd and a few years later moved him as manager to Hill Top Farm where he lived with his family and worked until his retirement.

William Heelis and Ann Preston
folk dancing at Hill Top, *c.*1930

Beatrix Potter and Tom Storey
with a prize ewe

Beatrix Potter
at Keswick Show

Troutbeck Park Farm today
(*Mike Williams*)

Examples of early
Peter Rabbit merchandise

Although Beatrix's preoccupation with farming had interrupted her flow of books, she kept in regular touch with her publishers, discussing the progress of the merchandise that was being made from the characters in her books and the constant reprints of the books themselves. Her following in America was growing very quickly and each spring saw an increasing number of American admirers in Sawrey, visits that Beatrix encouraged, enjoying the unaccustomed praise and enthusiasm: 'You come because you understand the books, and love the same old tales that I do – not from any impertinent curiosity.' The end of 1927 brought to Castle Cottage an American publisher, Alexander McKay, who came to see if he could persuade Beatrix to do a new book to satisfy the obvious demand. Two years later his American firm, David McKay, published *The Fairy Caravan*, a collection of short tales about a travelling circus that Beatrix had been writing for her own amusement for a number of years. To the great delight of many Sawrey residents the animals she featured in the book were those from Hill Top or ones belonging to her neighbours and they recognised that she had used the village and its surroundings as

Stoney Lane, Sawrey,
from *The Fairy Caravan*

the inspiration for the illustrations. Beatrix, however, felt *The Fairy Caravan* to be too autobiographical and revealing for publication in England by Frederick Warne, ('I am shy about publishing that stuff in London') and the book remained available only in its American edition until 1952, nine years after Beatrix's death.

Meanwhile Beatrix's talent for farm and land management was producing amazing results. Through her close friendship with the late Canon Hardwicke Rawnsley, whom she had met at Wray Castle on her very first visit to the Lake District, she had become a strong supporter of the work of the National Trust which Rawnsley co-founded in 1895. Beatrix was particularly interested in land preservation, in preventing the break-up of large estates and the destruction of old cottages, in stopping the building of cheap bungalows alongside quiet Lake District roads, and in ensuring the continued breeding and maintaining of Herdwick sheep on the farms in the district. She sent subscriptions to various National Trust appeals but she also contributed in a practical way, on one occasion raising money to save a strip of the foreshore of Windermere from building developers by selling a number of animal watercolours to admirers of her work in America.

From *The Fairy Caravan*

Hardwicke Rawnsley with Beatrix Potter
and her father

In 1930 Beatrix entered into a remarkable partnership with the National Trust. She bought the 2,500 acre Monk Coniston Estate and offered half of it to the Trust at the price she paid for it as soon as they were able to raise the money, promising that the other half would come to them after her death. The Trust raised the money quite quickly and they then asked Beatrix to look after the estate for them until such time as they could take it over. For the next seven years, as well as keeping her own farms and property under control, Beatrix managed the entire Monk Coniston Estate, collecting rents from the many cottages and farms, organising repairs to buildings and fences, and supervising the felling and planting of trees. In everything she was supported by Willie who was responsible for keeping the accounts and attending to any legal problems. It was not until early 1937, when Beatrix was well into her seventy-first year, that she handed their part of the estate back to the National Trust on the appointment of their first Lake District Land Agent, Bruce Thompson.

Some of the Monk Coniston Estate farms today *(Mike Williams)*

(above) High Yewdale

(right) Low Yewdale

(left) High Park

Beatrix Potter with her dogs, Chuleh and Tzusee, in 1936

Beatrix Potter,
September 1942, aged 76
(Reginald Hart)

The coming of the Second World War brought a renewal of the difficulties experienced by farmers only twenty years before. This time Beatrix and Willie were older and less able to cope, but they did what they could, Willie as reserve policeman and serving on the War Agricultural Committee, Beatrix taking the chair at Herdwick Sheepbreeders Association meetings and even allowing her precious Hill Top to be lived in by her cousin and family whose own house had been commandeered by the army.

Beatrix was dismayed by the lengthening war, and the many years she had spent out on the fells in all weathers was beginning to affect her health. The winter came early in 1943 and by the middle of November the snow had already reached the bottom of the Lake District fells. Beatrix had been ill in bed for some weeks with bronchitis and now her heart was troubling her. She was tired and worn out: 'But if an old person of 77 continues to play these games – well it can be done once too often.' Three days before Christmas Beatrix Potter died, her devoted husband by her bedside.

Hill Top porch today
(Cressida Pemberton-Pigott)

From *The Tale of Tom Kitten*

With the exception of a few small bequests, Beatrix left everything in her will to Willie for his lifetime, stipulating that after his death all her property should go to the National Trust. There were over 4,000 acres of land, including the rest of the Monk Coniston Estate, and numerous cottages and farms. She instructed that her house property and her farms should be let at moderate rents and that the landlord's flock on the fell farms should continue to be of the pure Herdwick breed. Hill Top was not to be let to anyone and the rooms and furnishings in it 'should be kept in their present condition'. Beatrix left a detailed list of where each item should stand and which of her best pieces in Castle Cottage should be moved to Hill Top for preservation.

A 1936 Christmas card design
by Beatrix Potter

Mrs Beckett, her son David and Mrs Preston
at Hill Top in 1902 *(Beatrix Potter)*

From *The Tale of Jemima Puddle-Duck*

William Heelis died less than two years later and in his will he stipulated that his property, including his office in Hawkshead (now The Beatrix Potter Gallery), should be added to Beatrix's gift to the National Trust.

On 1 November 1946 Hill Top Farm was let on a joint tenancy to Tom Storey and his son, Geoff. When Tom retired he moved into a house in Sawrey village where he lived until his death in 1986 at the age of ninety. Geoff took over the farm and held it until his untimely death in October 1988, not long before his own retirement. The farm has now been re-let.

Hill Top Farm today (*Mike Williams*)

Earlier in 1946, the National Trust had opened the house at Hill Top to the public and the crowds of admiring visitors have been streaming up the flagstone garden path ever since. Hill Top is a treasure trove for the Potter enthusiast. The rooms are filled with reminders of the stories that have given so much pleasure throughout the century – among them the dolls that were the models for Lucinda and Jane, the dresser past which Anna Maria ran with her stolen dough, the longcase clock from the tailor of Gloucester's kitchen. The garden of Hill Top evokes memories of Tom Kitten and the mischievous family of Mrs Tabitha Twitchit, a short walk into the village and you are on your way to tea with Duchess and Ribby or off to market with Pigling Bland and Alexander. Whichever way you turn the spirit and presence of Beatrix Potter lives on.

Hill Top garden path today
(*Cressida Pemberton-Pigott*)

Sawrey main street today (*Mike Williams*)

From *The Tale of Tom Kitten*

From *The Tale of Tom Kitten*

Hill Top garden gate today
(*Norwyn Photographics*)

Tour of the House

With the exception of the extension to the west, built in 1906 to house Beatrix Potter's farm manager, Hill Top dates from the late seventeenth century. It is a characteristic example of Lakeland vernacular architecture, with random stone walls and slate roof.

The Entrance Hall

This room retains its robust stone-flagged floor. The range illustrated in the 'little books' was later removed, but an identical one was found and installed in 1983. The room was repapered in 1987 with a screen-printed copy of a wallpaper hung by Beatrix Potter in 1906, covering the ceiling as well as the walls.

Displayed above a spinning-wheel to the left of the fireplace is a chimney crane and clockwork roasting-jack, an iron balance, two powder flasks and a warming-pan. The last, unusual in that it was intended to hold hot water rather than coals, belonged to Beatrix Potter's grandmother. A collection of horse brasses hangs above the fireplace, while on the mantelshelf are late nineteenth-century Doulton jugs and mugs alongside a late eighteenth-century Staffordshire bust of John Wesley. To the right of the fireplace are Beatrix Potter's hat and clogs which she often wore. The 'rag' rug in front of the fire is of a traditional type made in the Lake District.

The Georgian-style dresser may have been bought new in 1906 and is illustrated in *The Tale of Samuel Whiskers*. On the higher

From *The Tale of Samuel Whiskers*

From *The Tale of Samuel Whiskers*

Hill Top kitchen range today
(Geoffrey Frosh)

Clogs often worn by Beatrix Potter resting against the spinning wheel
(Geoffrey Frosh)

shelves are two Chinese early nineteenth-century tureen stands and an octagonal saucer dish, all in blue and white with Chinese landscapes, and two Staffordshire creamware bowls, one with portraits of George III and Queen Charlotte, the other with one of Lord Nelson. On a lower shelf are five scalloped Chinese plates, c.1700, painted with flowers and butterflies. The Kangxi teapot is Staffordshire, c.1840.

An oak press cupboard dated 1667 stands opposite the fireplace; it carries a Chinese ginger jar and an English cream jug of Chinese pattern, and a late eighteenth-century Liverpool creamware bowl decorated with transfer prints of pheasants and garden scenes. On the wall above is a set of plates transfer-printed in blue with animals and birds drawn by Rupert Potter.

The oak longcase clock is featured in *The Tailor of Gloucester*. It was made c.1785 by Thomas Barrow of Stockport, and has an exceptionally fine painted dial by James Wilson of Birmingham (d.1809). The mahogany chairs of Chippendale type appear frequently in Beatrix Potter's books.

Two small paintings hang to the right of the window: *Malin Head, Donegal* and *Holy Island* by Lord Leighton, PRA (1830–96). The stout beam which supports the ceiling carries an eel spear and nineteenth-century percussion-cap shotgun.

From *The Tailor of Gloucester*

One of Rupert Potter's
plate designs

The dresser and clock at Hill Top today *(Cressida Pemberton-Pigott)*

23

The Parlour

The imposing marble chimneypiece in the Adam manner was introduced by Beatrix Potter and strikes a curious note in this modest little parlour. On the mantelshelf, below a convex Regency mirror and a pair of Wedgwood floral transfer plates, are a pair of Staffordshire greyhounds with hares (*c.*1850) and an English double-handled pottery mug with oriental decoration (probably early Mason ware, *c.*1800).

The corner cupboard in the Parlour
(Geoffrey Frosh)

Furniture in this room includes a nineteenth-century mahogany card table, upon which is a fine rosewood writing box inlaid with mother-of-pearl; a rosewood worktable of *c.*1820; a Japanese *tansu*, or parquetry cabinet, decorated with *zaiku* panels from Hakone, near Tokyo; a prie-dieu or prayer chair of mahogany upholstered in yellow brocade (*c.*1840); and a set of four upholstered spoonback chairs in the French taste (*c.*1870).

The mid-eighteenth-century hanging corner cupboard contains English and Chinese porcelain, mostly *c.*1750–1850; the large teapot and matching plate on the second shelf are Derby, *c.*1810–20; the Edward VII coronation teapot dates from 1902 and is illustrated in *The Tale of the Pie and The Patty-Pan*. On the worktable below the cupboard is an unusual red box with a central panel of a Grecian woman and child set among wax impressions of classical gemstones.

To the left of the window hangs the Potter family's coat of arms (*dexter*: Potter quartering Moore; *sinister*: Crompton). It was through the Cromptons that Beatrix Potter had family associations with the Lake District, and as a child she was particularly attached to her Crompton grandmother. The circular watercolour of an *Arcadian Landscape*, above the coat of arms, is by W. R. Buckley (*fl.*1840–5).

To the right of the window are two oil paintings: *Hunting Scene*, signed 'R.M.A. 1865'; and *Ox Cart in Snow* by F. Koschny. The other oil paintings are, continuing clockwise: *Entrance to Loch Katrine* by Charlotte Nasmyth (*fl.*1840–62); three coastal scenes by John Brett, ARA (1830–1902) of *Falmouth Harbour* (1883), *Newhaven* (1883) *and Robin Hood's Bay* (1890); *Rydal Water* by W. L Turner, dated 1899; and *Swiss Cattle* by Randolph Caldecott (1846–86).

The large wall cupboard houses part of Beatrix Potter's collection of books, brought from Castle Cottage. Two of the photographs on display were taken at agricultural shows; in one of them she is with her shepherd Thomas Storey and a prize-winning sheep.

From *The Tale of the Pie and The Patty-Pan*

The Parlour
(Geoffrey Frosh)

Staircase and Landing

The stair-rail and balusters, familiar from illustrations in the books, are probably eighteenth-century. The large canvas, *Thanksgiving after the Flood*, is by the Genoese painter Giovanni Castiglione (1616–70); in the foreground pairs of animals are tended by Noah's son, while in the distance Noah himself is offering a sacrifice to God. Opposite hangs a late copy of Gainsborough's *The Hon. Mrs Graham*.

On the half-landing is an alabaster *Reading Girl*, after a larger work in marble by the Italian sculptor Pietro Magni (1817–77). The walnut-veneered longcase clock, which appears in *The Tale of Samuel Whiskers*, was made by Schofield's, of Rochdale.

Above the early eighteenth-century carved oak chest on the landing is a watercolour of *Two Girls on a Jetty*, painted in 1884 by George Dunlop Leslie, RA (1835–1921). The oil painting on the right-hand wall, *Colley and Pups*, is signed G.W. Horlor, 1865. The stair carpet and landing rug of traditional Turkish design was woven to recreate the character of those in *The Tale of Samuel Whiskers*.

Beatrix Potter's Bedroom

This bedroom was used on her first visits to Hill Top. The mid-seventeenth-century four-poster bed with a patchwork quilt was introduced later, when she moved to nearby Castle Cottage.

The limestone fireplace and carved wood mantel – inscribed with the date 1934 and initials 'W H B' – were put in by Beatrix

From *The Tale of Samuel Whiskers*

The half-landing today
(Geoffrey Frosh)

From *The Tale of Samuel Whiskers*

The landing at Hill Top today
(Geoffrey Frosh)

Potter's husband, William Heelis, who carved the mantel to commemorate their twenty-first wedding anniversary.

Opposite the fireplace, a seventeenth-century oak chest supports a Bible box in which Beatrix Potter's Bible is displayed. Above hangs a set of three gouache pictures of birds, by or after Samuel Dixon of Dublin (*fl.*1748–64). The chest is flanked by a pair of William and Mary oak chairs with original caned seats.

To the left of the window is an ebonized cabinet-on-stand, painted in imitation of oriental lacquerwork. The eighteenth-century piece to the right of the window consists of a number of Japanese lacquer panels fitted together asymmetrically to form a cabinet.

Also in this room is a showcase containing nineteenth-century dolls of which a flaxen-haired one is said to have been used as a model for Lucinda in *The Tale of Two Bad Mice*.

Dolls that belonged to Beatrix Potter
(Geoffrey Frosh)

The Bedroom *(Geoffrey Frosh)*

Cotton brocade bed hanging embroidered by her *(Geoffrey Frosh)*

The Treasure Room

Beatrix Potter used this small room to display her collection of mementoes and curios. Most of the pieces are housed in a mid-nineteenth-century ebonized showcase inlaid with satinwood, standing alongside an 1830s walnut davenport. The collection consists of china, trinkets, pendants, bracelets, and other objects of *virtu*. It includes a set of miniature bronze figures of characters from the books; a black saltglaze teapot of *c.*1830 (Staffordshire); two eighteenth-century Dresden porcelain jars; and some examples of Wedgwood 'jasper' and 'basalt' ware – a blue and green cornucopia, and a pair of black spillvases with a frieze of nymphs in white relief. The porcelain mug decorated with flowers was painted by William Billingsley who was associated with the Pinxton factory in Derbyshire between 1796 and 1799.

Above the showcase is a late eighteenth-century painting of *The Old Ferry Hotel, Windermere*, flanked by oval flower studies of *Primula farinosa* and *Rosa gallica* 'Versicolor' by Valentine Bartholomew (1799–1879).

More items of Wedgwood jasper ware can be seen on the mid-nineteenth-century ebonized and ivory-inlaid cabinet by the door. The shelf carries a green and yellow bulb bowl and a pair of green urn-shaped *pot pourri* jars with candle holders; below is a pair of lilac urns either side of a larger black basalt urn.

The doll's house, although not the one featured in *The Tale of Two Bad Mice*, does contain the very doll's house food that Hunca Munca and Tom Thumb stole.

Above the doll's house is a pair of coloured prints of drawings by the children's book illustrator Randolph Caldecott (1846–86). Beatrix Potter refers to the prints in a letter of 1942: 'The pretty maid hanging out the clothes was the Caldecotts' maid at the house in Surrey'.

On either side are canvaswork hangings which are said to have been made by Beatrix Potter on the embroidery frame to be seen in the Sitting Room.

A display of her curios and mementoes
(Geoffrey Frosh)

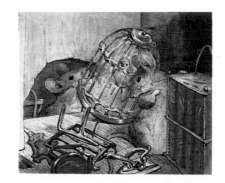

From *The Tale of Two Bad Mice*

The doll's house in the Treasure Room
(Geoffrey Frosh)

The Sitting Room
(Geoffrey Frosh)

Beatrix Potter (with toy rabbit)
and her cousin, Alice Crompton Potter

The Sitting Room

The original seventeenth-century stone fireplace survives, framed by a wooden mantel which probably dates from the early eighteenth century. On the mantelshelf is a pair of richly gilt perforated pastille burners of Derby manufacture, *c.*1820.

The mahogany bureau-bookcase of *c.*1770 contains English china collected by Beatrix Potter – including a dolls' Staffordshire tea service of *c.*1830 and a Wedgwood tea-set portraying characters from her books. A number of jugs are of the early nineteenth-century type popularly known as Pratt ware. The small figures of a Turk and a girl date from about 1780 and are probably of Leeds manufacture, copying a Meissen design.

Various photographs of Beatrix Potter are displayed here: in one she is with her cousin Alice Crompton Potter, at about five years of age and holding a toy rabbit; in another she is with her father, Rupert Potter, and her brother, Bertram.

The remaining furniture, all in mahogany, includes a mid-eighteenth-century chest-of-drawers; and a square piano by Clementi, *c.*1810.

Among the pictures in this room is a charming watercolour by Beatrix Potter entitled *Spring*. This hangs to the right of the window, above an oil painting of *Langdale Pikes from Low Wood* by James Francis Williams (1785–1846). The other pictures are, continuing clockwise, *Château de Thun*, a Swiss watercolour dated 1847; *Fields at Sunset*, painted by Bertram Potter in 1905; a late nineteenth-century study in oils of *A Rocky Coast*; a watercolour view of *Whitehall* in 1890 by Herbert Menzies Marshall (1841–1913), and another of *S. Giorgio Maggiore, Venice*; two *Sunsets* in pastel by Bertram Potter; *Loch Ainost, Skye*, a watercolour of 1874 by Spencer Vincent (d.1910); two watercolours by George Arthur Fripp (1813–96) of *Loch Ness* and *Glencoe*; a nineteenth-century *View of a Lake*; two *Coastal Scenes* in oil by Lord Leighton, PRA (1830–96); and a watercolour study of *Fossils and Minerals* dated 1889 by Kate Mary Whitley.

The New Room

Beatrix Potter called this the New Room because it was part of the extension she built on to Hill Top in 1906. It was here that she did her writing. William Heelis put up the neo-Classical panelling (apparently never finished) to display some large landscapes by Bertram Potter.

The furniture which Beatrix Potter brought into the room includes an oak bureau-bookcase of *c.*1725 (to the right of the fireplace); a cane-seated bentwood armchair; a walnut easy chair of *c.*1850; an Edwardian mahogany card table of 'envelope' design; and a miniature bow-fronted commode with marble top, in the Louis XV style. Her copy of Gerard's *Herbal* (1633) is displayed in a cabinet specially made for it in 1989.

Other pieces are from the small study she furnished for herself at Troutbeck Park Farm: a red walnut bureau of *c.*1730; three mahogany Chippendale chairs; a rosewood writing-box; and an Edwardian display cabinet full of the curious china and glass which she collected at Troutbeck Park.

The New Room
(Geoffrey Frosh)

Stoney Lane from above Hill Top today
(Mike Williams)

From *The Tale of
Samuel Whiskers*

The Garden

In many of the illustrations to her story books, Beatrix Potter revealed her love and knowledge of traditional cottage garden plants. She herself planned and executed the layout of Hill Top's garden, which is best seen in late spring and early summer when the flowering borders are in full bloom. She illustrated it with particular vividness in *The Tale of Tom Kitten*, and this book has been used in conjunction with other references – in her letters, a few surviving contemporary photographs, and the memories of local residents – to inform today's gardeners as to how it should look.

In her letters, Beatrix Potter referred to azaleas, phlox, roses, saxifrage, hollyhocks, lilies, London Pride, rock plants and fruit trees. All these are grown at Hill Top today in varieties known in her time, clustered together and rather haphazardly interspersed with vegetables, to retain the cottage garden atmosphere she loved.

From *The Tale of Tom Kitten*

From *The Tale of Pigling Bland*

Hill Top garden today